REAL WORLD DATA

GRAPHING PLANET EARTH

Elizabeth Miles

www.heinemann.co.uk/library
Visit our website to find out more information about **Heinemann Library** books.

To order:

 ☎ Phone 44 (0) 1865 888066

🖹 Send a fax to 44 (0) 1865 314091

💻 Visit the Heinemann Bookshop at www.heinemann.co.uk/library to browse our catalogue and order online.

Heinemann Library is an imprint of Pearson Education Limited, a company incorporated in England and Wales having its registered office at Edinburgh Gate, Harlow, Essex, CM20 2JE – Registered company number: 00872828
Heinemann Library is a registered trademark of Pearson Education Limited
Text © Pearson Education Ltd 2009
First published in hardback in 2009
Paperback edition first published in 2009
The moral rights of the proprietor have been asserted.

Edited by Nancy Dickmann and Rachel Howells
Designed by Victoria Bevan and Geoff Ward
Original illustrations© Pearson Education Ltd
Illustrations by Geoff Ward
Picture research by Hannah Taylor
Originated by Modern Age
Printed and bound in China by Leo Paper Group

ISBN 978 0 431 02946 7 (hardback)
13 12 11 10 09
10 9 8 7 6 5 4 3 2 1

ISBN 978 0 431 02960 3 (paperback)
13 12 11 10 09
10 9 8 7 6 5 4 3 2 1

British Library Cataloguing in Publication Data
Miles, Elizabeth,
Graphing Planet Earth. - (Real world data)
551.4'1'0728
A full catalogue record for this book is available from the British Library.

Acknowledgements
The publishers would like to thank the following for permission to reproduce photographs:
©ardea.com p. 21 (Johan de Meester); ©Corbis pp. 8 (Roger Ressmeyer/NASA), 18 (Arctic-Images); ©Getty Images pp. 12 (Kolchi Kamoshida), 22 (AFP/Arif Ali); ©Photolibrary p. 14 (Australian Only); ©Science Photo Library pp. 4 (Mehau Kulyk), 6 (Detley Van Ravenswaay), 10 (Roger Harris), 17 (B. Murton), 16 (Martin Bond); ©Still Pictures p. 15 (H. Baesemann).

Cover photograph of river deltas in Borneo, reproduced with permission of ©Science Photo Library (M-SAT LTD).

The publishers would like to thank Harold Pratt for his assistance in the preparation of this book.

Every effort has been made to contact copyright holders of any material reproduced in this book. Any omissions will be rectified in subsequent printings if notice is given to the publishers.

Disclaimer
All the internet addresses (URLs) given in this book were valid at time of going to press. However, due to the dynamic nature of the Internet, some addresses may have changed, or sites may have changed or ceased to exist since publication. While the author and publishers regret any inconvenience this may cause readers, no responsibility for any such changes can be accepted by either the author or the publishers. It is recommended that adults supervise children on the Internet.

CONTENTS

Some words are printed in bold, **like this**. You can find out what they mean by looking in the glossary, on page 30.

Most scientists believe that the **Universe** began 15 billion years ago with an explosion called the Big Bang. In the first few seconds, tiny particles formed from the energy of the explosion. These later joined together to form atoms – the building blocks of **matter**. Everything we see is made of matter, from people, to mountains, to stars.

Billions of years after the Big Bang, swirling clouds of gas formed **galaxies**, such as our Milky Way galaxy. **Solar systems** with stars (such as our Sun) and **planets** (such as Earth) formed much later.

Earth

Earth probably began to form about 4,500 million years ago. At first it was just a spinning ball of hot liquid rock. As it cooled, the **atmosphere** formed and then the oceans appeared. The first simple life forms took a long time to develop, compared with all the other animal types that **evolved** faster afterwards. Animals on the land appeared about 300 million years ago. Human beings evolved only about 3 million years ago. It can be difficult to imagine how long it took for the Earth we know today to develop. Millions of years are difficult to grasp and compare.

This picture shows what the Big Bang might have looked like. Of course, there was no one to see it!

Tables and timelines

A table like the one below is helpful because it gathers together some of the most important events in the Earth's development. To help us see the order of events, a timeline is even more useful. In this timeline, major events since the Earth formed have been squashed into a single year. This helps us to imagine and compare the time it took for different things to happen. We can also see the size of the gaps between events.

What happened?	Millions of years ago (approximately)
Earth formed	4,500
Oceans first appeared on Earth	3,800
Life first appeared	3,500
First fish evolved	400
First amphibians evolved	365
First mammals evolved	200
Dinosaurs evolved	200
First birds evolved	160
First people lived on Earth	2

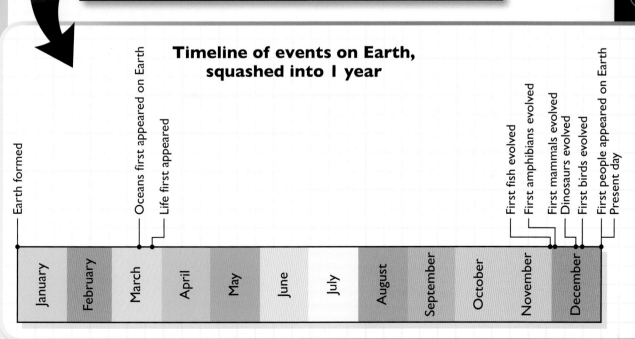

Timeline of events on Earth, squashed into 1 year

PLANET EARTH

Earth is a giant rocky object called a **planet**. It is one of a group of planets that **orbit** (travel around) the Sun. The Sun and its eight planets are together called the **Solar System**. Earth is the only planet in the Solar System where life exists. This is partly because it is just the right distance from the Sun. If it were closer to the Sun, it would be too hot for life; if it were further from the Sun, it would be too cold. For example, Venus is so hot, even metal would melt on its surface.

 Many of the planets of the solar system have their own moons. Over 60 moons orbit Jupiter! Saturn is circled by rings of orbiting dust, rocks, and ice.

The other planets

The planets are different in many other ways, too. For example, the **atmosphere** around Earth is made of the gases that people and most plants need to live. But Mars' atmosphere has too little **oxygen** for us to live there and Jupiter's atmosphere is poisonous. Some of the planets do not have a solid surface to live on. Underneath Jupiter's poisonous clouds, there is just a deep ocean of liquid hydrogen with no land.

Bar graphs

A bar graph uses vertical blocks, or bars, to show data. This bar graph shows the planets along the **x-axis**, in order of their distance from the Sun. The height of each bar shows the planet's average temperature. Set out visually like this, it is easy to spot a pattern. Mostly, the bars go down the further away a planet is from the Sun. However, Venus has a higher temperature than Mercury. There must be other things that affect the temperature of the planets, such as what they are made of.

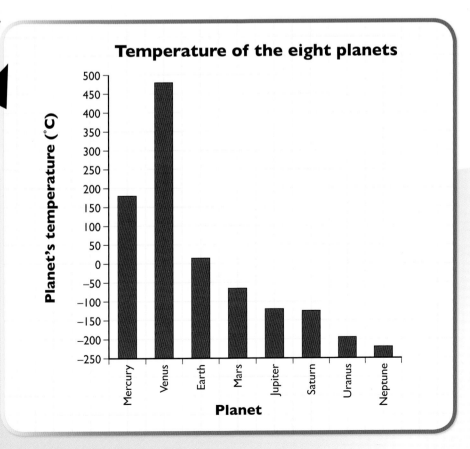

Temperature of the eight planets

Planet's temperature (°C) vs. Planet (Mercury, Venus, Earth, Mars, Jupiter, Saturn, Uranus, Neptune)

Earth is round, so why doesn't everything on it fall off? It is because of a powerful, invisible force called **gravity**. Gravity is the force that pulls everything towards the centre of Earth. The force of Earth's gravity stops us from falling off the **planet**. It stops other things, including the **atmosphere**, from floating away. The force of gravity makes snowflakes fall to the ground and rivers flow downhill.

It is difficult to escape the power of the Earth's gravity. For example, a thrown ball only goes so high before it falls back down. A lot of energy is needed to launch a heavy spacecraft out of gravity's grasp.

Gravity and mass

Every object has gravity and pulls things towards it. The greater the **mass** an object has, the more powerful its force of gravity. An object with a small mass has such a weak gravitational force, we do not feel it. The Sun is so massive that its powerful gravity keeps Earth and other planets in **orbit** around it. The Moon has a smaller mass and its force of gravity is much weaker. It cannot even hold an atmosphere around it. Each planet has a different mass, so gravity is more or less powerful on each planet.

In space, away from the pull of Earth's gravity, astronauts feel weightless.

Gravity and weight

Weight is a measure of gravity. The greater the force of a planet's gravity, the heavier it makes any objects on its surface. For example, a person standing on Earth would be heavier than if they stood on the Moon.

How much would you weigh on the Moon?

You can work out how much you would weigh elsewhere in the Solar System. All you need to do is to multiply your weight in kilograms (on Earth) by each of the numbers below.

Moon	–	0.17
Mars	–	0.4
Jupiter	–	2.5
Sun	–	28

Double bar charts

Like a bar chart, a double bar chart helps compare information. However, in a double bar chart, it is possible to include information for more than one place or time. This double bar chart shows how much a person and an elephant would weigh on the Moon and on different planets.

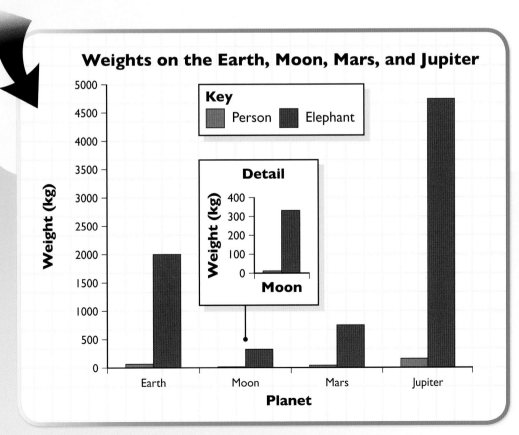

Weights on the Earth, Moon, Mars, and Jupiter

Key
Person   Elephant

Detail

EARTH'S STRUCTURE

Earth began as a spinning ball of hot rock. The rock was so hot that it was molten. Very slowly, the outer surface of the Earth cooled and the rock became solid. This cool outer layer is called the **crust**.

Under the crust of rock beneath our feet, there is still a mass of swirling, hot material. This layer is called the **mantle**.

Sometimes, some of the hot material from the mantle escapes to the surface of the Earth. It oozes through **faults** in the crust or explodes out in volcanic eruptions.

Below the mantle, lies an outer core. This is made of hot liquid metal. The centre of the Earth is called the inner core. Here, the metal is solid but also extremely hot.

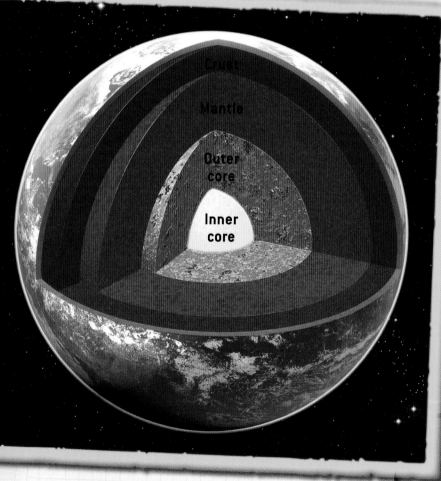

Crust

Mantle

Outer core

Inner core

Hot rocks
It would take three to four months to walk down a tunnel to the centre of the Earth. It would be impossible to survive the trip because you would burn up as soon as you got below the crust.

 This cross-section of the Earth shows the layers that lie beneath the surface.

Scale problems

Because the layers of the Earth vary so much in thickness, it is difficult to show them to the correct scale in an illustration or a graph. If the crust were drawn as 1mm thick, the mantle would have to be drawn as 480 mm thick and wouldn't fit on the page! The bar chart below helps to show the size difference between the layers. A part of the chart has been pulled out and enlarged. If this had not been done, the bar for the crust would be impossible to see. A table like the one below shows the actual thickness of each layer.

Section	Thickness
crust	6–30 km (4–19 miles)
mantle	2,900 km (1,800 miles)
outer core	2,200 km (1,370 miles)
inner core	1,250 km (780 miles)

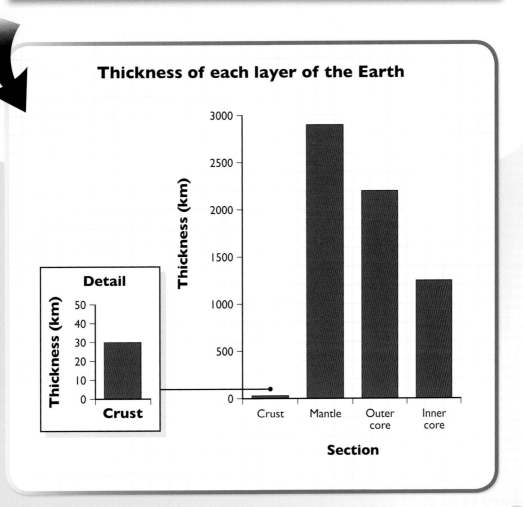

Thickness of each layer of the Earth

CRASHING PLATES

The Earth's **crust** is made up of several pieces, called **tectonic plates**. Although these plates did once fit together like jigsaw pieces, they are always moving about. This movement happens because they are floating on the soft **mantle** below. The soft mantle moves slowly, and it carries the plates along with it. Some plates slide past one another. Others collide or pull apart.

This tectonic plate movement is slow – about 1 cm (1/2 inch) a year. But it can still have dramatic effects: where plates collide, rocks crumple up into vast mountain ranges. Where plates pull away from each other, faults, deep ocean trenches, valleys, and volcanoes can appear. When plates slide past each other, they can get stuck. Pressure builds until suddenly they start to move again. The ground shakes and cracks, and there can be an **earthquake**.

 Earthquake damage in Ojiya, Japan in October 2004. The earthquake measured 6.8 on the Richter Scale.

Earthquakes

Earthquakes are often so small that no one notices them. Others are so great that buildings collapse, bridges fall, and the ground cracks open. During an earthquake, **vibrations** travel through the Earth's crust. They spread out in a circular pattern from the centre of the earthquake (the epicentre).

The movements are strongest at the epicentre, and get weaker further away.

The power of an earthquake is called its magnitude. Scientists describe this by using the Richter Scale. The scale goes from 0 (the weakest) to 9.5 (the most powerful ever recorded).

How strong?

Only a few earthquakes are strong enough to cause a lot of damage. This double bar chart shows the number of earthquakes of different magnitudes. Earthquakes of more than 6.0 can be devastating. However, there are not many of these powerful earthquakes each year. Most earthquakes range from 3.0 to 4.9. They can make things rattle and shake.

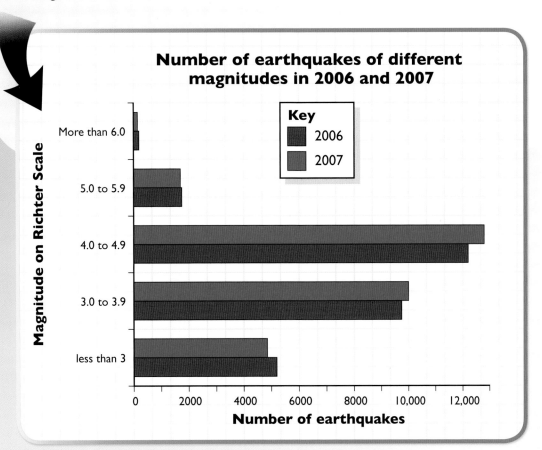

THE ATMOSPHERE

The Earth has another layer beyond the crust. The **atmosphere**, which is made up of gases, surrounds the Earth. It stretches about 700 kilometres (435 miles) up into the sky, and then gradually thins into space. The atmosphere keeps the Earth warm. Like a blanket, it holds in some of the Earth's heat. It also protects us from harmful rays given out by the Sun.

Without the atmosphere, there would be no life on Earth. The atmosphere provides human beings, plants, and animals with the gases they need to live. Human beings need to breathe in **oxygen**, while most plants need to take in **carbon dioxide**.

Water in the air

When talking about the contents of the atmosphere, we often leave out **water vapour**. This is water that exists as an invisible gas. It is difficult to include a figure for water vapour because the amount in the air varies a lot. For example, in hot, sticky weather, there is a lot of water vapour in the atmosphere. In cold, dry weather, there is far less.

 Clouds in Earth's atmosphere are visible from space.

When water vapour cools it changes from a gas to a liquid. This is called **condensing**. It forms visible water droplets. Clouds are made of these droplets, and when the droplets are big enough, they fall from the clouds as rain. In this way, the atmosphere gives us weather.

 Storm clouds can stretch more than 6,000 metres (20,000 feet) above the Earth's surface.

Pie charts

Pie charts help to show parts of a whole. They are the best way to show how something is divided up. This pie chart shows the gases that make up dry air. The biggest "slice" of the pie is nitrogen. This shows that nitrogen makes up the main part of air. The oxygen we need to live is only a small part of it. The key shows what each colour means on the pie chart.

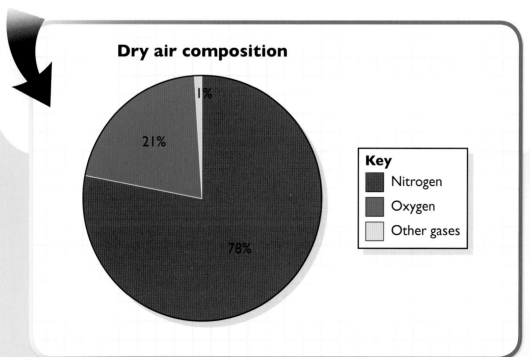

Dry air composition

1%
21%
78%

Key
Nitrogen
Oxygen
Other gases

Most of the surface of the Earth is made up of either vast oceans or huge areas of land. There are five major oceans: the Pacific, Atlantic, Indian, Southern, and Arctic. There are seven major landmasses, called **continents**. These are Africa, Antarctica, Asia, Australia, Europe, North America, and South America.

The thickness of the **crust** is thinner under the oceans than where the continents are. The edges of the continents slope down into the oceans to form continental shelves. Here the water is only about 200 m (120 miles) deep. The land then slopes downwards to form the vast ocean floor, where the deep oceans sit like giant puddles.

 Ocean waves break along the coasts, where land and sea meet.

A blue planet

Earth is often called the "blue planet" because of its oceans. Far more of the Earth's surface is covered in water than most people realize. Much of it has not yet been explored. Beneath the water's surface there are mountains, valleys, and plains. Earth's longest mountain range is at the bottom of the Atlantic Ocean. The deepest place on Earth is the Mariana Trench in the Pacific Ocean. It is so deep, you could put Mount Everest in it and there would still be over 2,000 metres (1,200 miles) of water above the mountain's peak.

 This erupting volcano is on the ocean floor.

Water and land

A pie chart makes it easy to see how much of the surface of the Earth is covered by water. Many pie charts use suitable colours to represent the things they show. This one uses green for dry land and blue for water. On a pie chart, the biggest section usually starts at the mid, top point (where 12 would be on a clock).

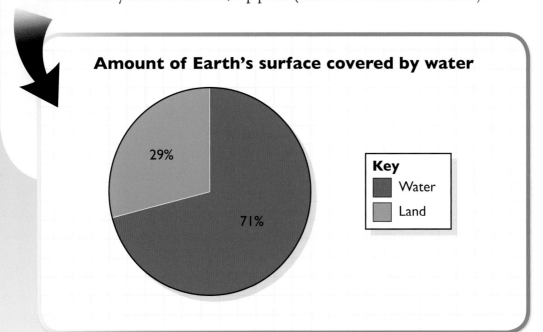

Amount of Earth's surface covered by water

29%

71%

Key
- Water
- Land

The Earth **rotates** as it travels round the sun. This means that it spins around its **axis** – an imaginary line that goes through the middle of the Earth, from the North Pole to the South Pole. This rotation makes it seem as if the Sun rises in the morning and sets in the evening.

The Earth takes nearly 24 hours to rotate once. During that time, part of the world turns to face the Sun, and day begins. The opposite side turns away from the Sun, and night falls. At any one time about half of the Earth faces the Sun. So, while it is morning on one side of the Earth, it is evening on the other.

Polar regions

Places near the **poles** are unusual. They are lit by the Sun all day for six months of the year. The Sun never sets during these months. This is because the Earth's axis is tilted. Each pole is brightly lit for six months when it is tilted towards the Sun. Then it is left in the dark for six months when it is tilted away.

 Places like Iceland are lit by the Sun all day for six months. They are called the "lands of the midnight sun".

Time zones

Because it is always a different time of day in different parts of the world, the world has been divided into **time zones**. There is a time zone for each hour, and as you travel east round the world, you need to put your clock forward. Time zones generally follow national or regional boundaries. It is easier for people to work together if they are in the same time zone. A table can show the time in different cities. A time zone map of the world shows the boundaries between time zones. (The boundaries shown below are approximate, not actual.)

City	Time
Sydney	1:00 a.m.
Los Angeles	7:00 a.m.
New York	10:00 a.m.
London	3:00 p.m.
Moscow	6:00 p.m.
Singapore	10:00 p.m.

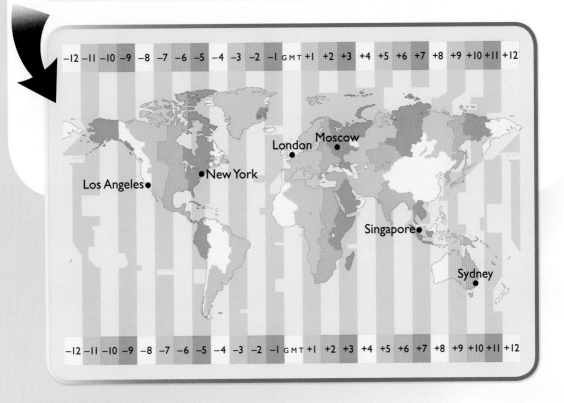

THE SEASONS

The Earth takes just over 365 days (about a year) to go once round the Sun. During this time the Earth's **axis** stays tilted in the same direction. The tilt means that for part of the year, the northern **hemisphere** of the Earth is closer to the Sun and the southern hemisphere is further away. Six months later, the southern hemisphere is tilted towards the Sun, while the northern hemisphere is tilted away from it.

This tilt means that some places get more heat and light from the Sun during one half of the year. They get less heat and light from the sun during the other half of the year.

The tilt of the Earth's axis and the Earth's orbit around the Sun creates the seasons. In places between the **poles** and the **equator**, there are four **seasons**:

- ✦ winter: when the place is tilted away from the Sun and temperatures are low
- ✦ spring: when the place begins to be tilted towards the Sun, and temperatures begin to rise
- ✦ summer: the place is tilted towards the Sun and temperatures are high
- ✦ autumn: when the place begins to be tilted away from the Sun, and temperatures begin to fall.

 As the Earth orbits the Sun, it also turns on its axis. The Earth's axis is not vertical – it leans.

 In low-lying places between the poles and the equator, snow usually only falls in winter.

Line graphs

Line graphs can show how something, such as temperature, changes over time. Dates or times are usually shown on the **x-axis**. The **y-axis** shows specific **data**, such as the average temperature in a certain month. Data is plotted using a point for each date, and a line joins the points. This graph shows average temperature by month in two cities; one in the northern hemisphere and one in the southern hemisphere. Each line shows a different city. You can see that when it is warm in Chicago, it is cold in Sydney.

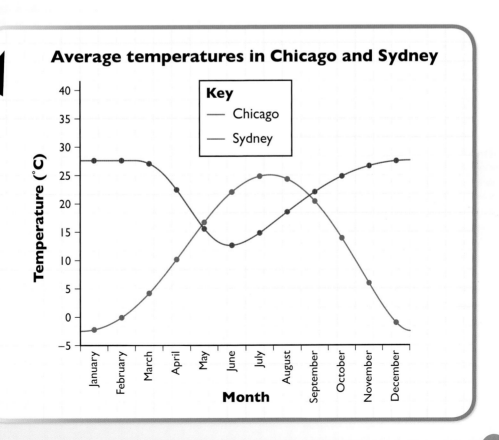

Average temperatures in Chicago and Sydney

Key
— Chicago
— Sydney

Temperature (°C) / Month

SEASONS AROUND THE WORLD

The tilt of the Earth means that places between the **equator** and **poles** have four **seasons** with different temperatures. Near the poles, the Earth's tilt means that temperatures vary far more. Long, cold winters are followed by short, mild summers.

The areas least affected by the Earth's tilt are the tropics – places on and near the equator. Because they are never tilted too far away from or towards the Sun, temperatures vary less. Different seasonal temperatures are hardly noticeable.

While the temperatures do not vary much in the tropics, the amount of rain does. Instead of summer and winter seasons, people in the tropics experience dry and wet seasons. The dry and rainy seasons are created by winds. In the rainy season, torrential rains fall, often causing floods.

 Floods in Pakistan in 2007 after heavy monsoon rains.

Temperatures around the world

By comparing the temperatures in three different parts of the world, you can see which are the most affected by seasons. This three-line graph compares temperatures in three places:

1 near the equator (Singapore)

2 near the South Pole (McMurdo in Antarctica)

3 between the equator and the North Pole (London).

By looking along each line, you can see how the temperatures vary in each place. This shows the change in the seasons. Before looking at the key, try guessing which line belongs to a place that has four distinct seasons. Remember to always check the scale on a graph carefully. For example, this one includes minus temperatures (temperatures below 0 degrees celsius).

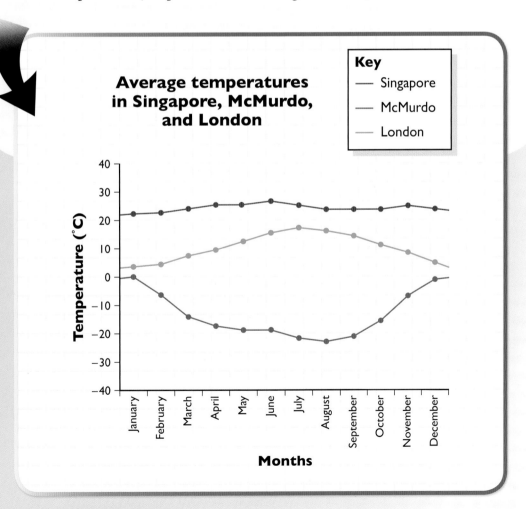

EARTH'S MOON

The Moon is Earth's nearest neighbour – about 384,400 kilometres (238,900 miles) away from Earth. The Moon travels with the Earth around the Sun. While doing so, it **orbits** the Earth.

It takes the Moon 27.3 days to travel round the Earth. The Moon also **rotates** once on its **axis** in the same period of time. This is why we always see the same side of the Moon. The other side is never seen from the Earth.

The moon takes just over 27 days to orbit the Earth.

Phases of the Moon

Like Earth, the Moon is round, and only half of it is lit by the Sun at a time. We see different amounts of the Moon's sunlit side as it orbits the Earth. When we cannot see any of its lit side, it is called a New Moon. During a Full Moon we can see the whole of its lit side.

A New Moon takes about two weeks to turn into a Full Moon, and another two weeks to turn back into a New Moon. While the Moon is growing into a Full Moon, it is said to be "waxing". While the Moon is shrinking into a New Moon it is said to be "waning". The different amounts of the Moon that we can see are called "**phases**". A full **lunar** month is the time it takes for us to see all of the Moon's phases (29.53 days).

Table or calendar?

Tables show the phases of the Moon in any year, so that you can find out when you will see a Full Moon, a New Moon, a First Quarter, or a Last Quarter. This table shows the phases of the Moon in November 2010. If the phases are labelled on a calendar, it is easy to remember when the different phases will appear.

Phases of the Moon in 2010

PHASE OF MOON	New Moon	First Quarter	Full Moon	Last Quarter
DATE IN NOVEMBER 2010	6th	13th	21st	28th

November 2010

Su	Mo	Tu	We	Th	Fr	Sa
	1	2	3	4	5	6
7	8	9	10	11	12	13
14	15	16	17	18	19	20
21	22	23	24	25	26	27
28	29	30				

TIDES

The Moon's **gravity** is fairly weak, but it has a powerful effect on the oceans. As it **orbits** the Earth, the Moon's gravity pulls at the oceans below. This makes the level of the oceans rise on two sides of the Earth, and fall on the other two sides of the Earth. We see this change as high and low **tides** along coastlines. Twice a day, as the Earth **rotates**, the sea level rises as a high tide, then falls as a low tide. Throughout each day, tides rise and fall around the world, as the Moon's gravity pulls on different parts of the Earth's oceans.

The oceans are affected by the sun's gravity, too. But the Sun's gravity has less of an effect because the Sun is much farther away. However, when the Sun, Moon, and Earth are in line, the combined pull of the Moon and Sun cause extra high and extra low tides. These are called spring tides.

When the Sun and Moon are at right angles to each other their forces of gravity are pulling the oceans in different directions. This makes the tides less extreme. They are called neap tides.

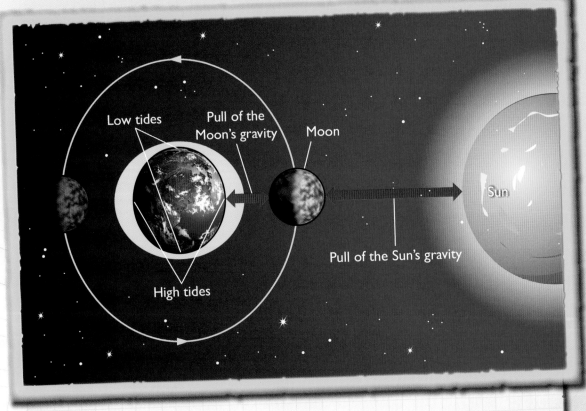

When the Sun, Moon, and Earth are in line, there are spring tides.

Time and tide

Sailors need to know the times of high and low tides to sail safely. Some coastal waters are too shallow to sail in at low tide. Many boats need a high tide to get in and out of harbours. A tide timetable provides a clear record of this information. It gives the times of the lowest and highest tides each day.

Time	Type of tide	Level of tide
5:17 a.m.	low	2.08 m (6.82 ft)
11:19 a.m.	high	5.32 m (17.45 ft)
5:36 p.m.	low	2.31 m (7.58 ft)
11:53 p.m.	high	5.42 m (17.78 ft)

To compare high and low tides, a bar graph is more useful. This bar graph clearly shows how the depth of water varies at different tides. The difference between high and low is much greater during a spring tide.

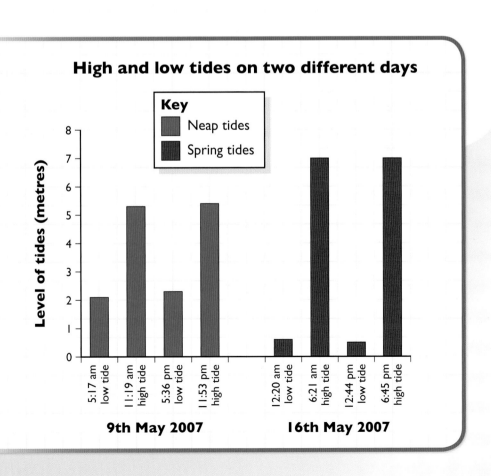

High and low tides on two different days

Key
- Neap tides
- Spring tides

Level of tides (metres)

5:17 am low tide | 11:19 am high tide | 5:36 pm low tide | 11:53 pm high tide

9th May 2007

12:20 am low tide | 6:21 am high tide | 12:44 pm low tide | 6:45 pm high tide

16th May 2007

Data is information about something. We often get important data as a mass of numbers, and it is difficult to make any sense of them. Graphs and charts are ways of displaying information visually. This helps us to see relationships and patterns in the data. Different types of graphs or charts are good for displaying different types of information.

Bar charts

Bar charts are a good way to compare amounts of different things. Bar charts have a **y-axis** showing the scale, and an **x-axis** showing the different types of information. When you are drawing graphs always label each axis and give your graph a title.

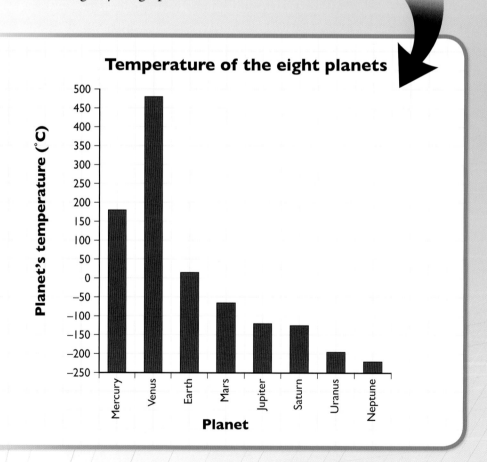

Pie charts

A pie chart shows information as different sized portions of a circle. They can help you compare **proportions**. When drawing a pie chart, you usually begin with the biggest portion at the "12 o'clock point" and then continue with the next sized portions in a clockwise order.

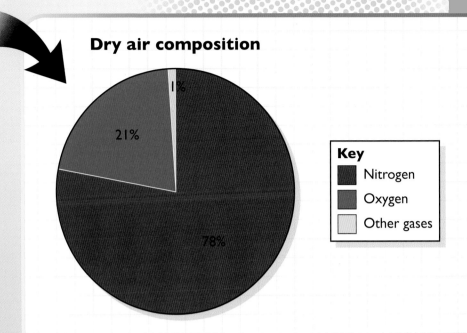

Dry air composition

1%

21%

78%

Key
- Nitrogen
- Oxygen
- Other gases

Line graphs

Line graphs use lines to join up points on a graph. They can be used to show how something changes over time. Several lines on one line graph mean that you can compare the overall pattern of several sets of data. Time, such as months, is usually shown on the x-axis.

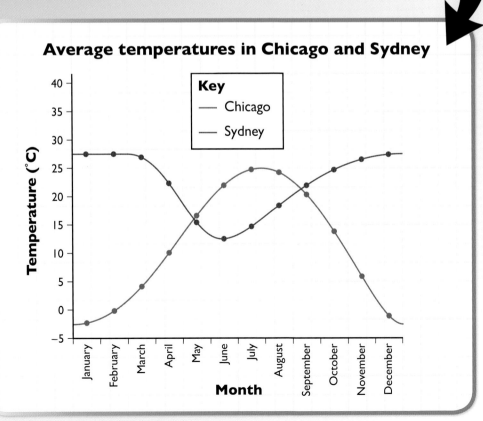

Average temperatures in Chicago and Sydney

Key
- Chicago
- Sydney

Temperature (°C)

Month

GLOSSARY

atmosphere layer of gases around a planet

axis imaginary line around which the Earth rotates

carbon dioxide gas that most plants need to live

condense change into a liquid

continent very large mass of land

core middle part of the Earth

crust the outer layer of the solid Earth

data information, often in the form of numbers

earthquake sudden movement of the Earth's surface

equator imaginary line around the Earth that divides the Earth into the northern and southern hemispheres

evolve to develop over time. New species of animals exist because of evolution.

fault break in the Earth's crust

galaxy very large group of stars

gravity force that pulls objects towards each other

hemisphere half of the Earth

lunar to do with the Moon

mantle layer inside the Earth, between the crust and the core

mass amount of matter in an object

matter something that takes up space, or a physical material

orbit the path an object in space (such as the Earth) takes around another object in space (such as the Sun)

oxygen the gas that people need to stay alive

phase how much of the Moon you can see

planet object, such as Earth, that travels around a star, such as our Sun

pole the furthest northern and southern points on Earth

proportion size of a group of data compared to other groups, or to the whole set of data

rotate to spin or go round like a wheel

season period of weather, such as winter

solar system group of planets and other objects, and the Sun they revolve around

tectonic plate piece of the Earth's crust, or shell

tide rise or fall in the ocean, most noticeably along coastlines

time zone area where all the clocks are set to read the same time

Universe everything that exists, including outer space and all that is in it

vibration quick to and fro movement

water vapour water in the form of a gas

weight a measure of the force of gravity on an object

x-axis horizontal line on a graph

y-axis vertical line on a graph

FURTHER INFORMATION

Books

Earth and Space: Mercury, Mars, and Other Inner Planets, Chris Oxlade
  (Rosen Central, 2007)

Eyewitness Project Books: Earth (Dorling Kindersley, 2008)

Planet Earth: Core and Crust, Amy Bauman (Ticktock Media Ltd, 2008)

The Universe: Earth, Stuart Clark (Heinemann Library, 2007)

Voyages Through Time: The Beginning, Peter Ackroyd (Dorling Kindersley, 2003)

Websites

The NASA website has information on the solar system.
  http://solarsystem.nasa.gov/planets

The US Naval Observatory website has information about the Moon's phases
  and phases of the Moon calendars.
  http://aa.usno.navy.mil

The US Geological Survey website has a "Top 10" list of earthquakes.
  http://earthquake.usgs.gov/eqcenter/top10.php

The Scripps Institution of Oceanography website looks at plate tectonics.
  www.sio.ucsd.edu/voyager/earth_puzzle

INDEX